D1682267

HARVEST
SEASON OF PROVISION

WORSHIP THROUGH THE SEASONS

DAVID M. EDWARDS

B&H PUBLISHING GROUP
NASHVILLE, TENNESSEE

Harvest: Season of Provision
Worship Through the Seasons Series
Copyright © 2006 by David M. Edwards
All Rights Reserved

ISBN 0-8054-4333-9
ISBN 13: 978-0-8054-4333-2
Broadman & Holman Publishers
Nashville, Tennessee
www.broadmanholman.com

Unless otherwise noted, all Scripture quotations have been taken from the Holman Christian Standard Bible® Copyright© 1999, 2000, 2002, 2003 by Holman Bible Publishers.

Other translations used include The Message (MSG) and the New King James Version (NKJV).

Dewey Decimal Classification: 242
Devotional Literature \ Worship

Printed in China
1 2 3 4 09 08 07 06

To Susan

Thank you for walking through life's seasons with me.

Love, David

Loving Shepherd of Thy sheep,
Keep thy lamb, in safety keep;
Nothing can Thy power withstand,
None can pluck me from Thy hand.

I would bless Thee every day,
Gladly all Thy will obey,
Like Thy blessed ones above,
Happy in Thy perfect love.

Loving Shepherd, ever near,
Teach Thy lamb Thy voice to hear;
Suffer not my steps to stray
From the straight and narrow way.

Where Thou leadest I would go,
Walking in Thy steps below,
Till before my Father's throne,
I shall know as I am known.

—Jane Leeson (1807–82)

INTRODUCTION

This is one of four books in a devotional series called *Worship Through the Seasons*. These seasonal books mirror the calendar year: Advent, Easter, Pentecost, Harvest. Rather than using a daily devotional template, I wanted to offer writings that would coincide with a particular time of the year and could be read and contemplated throughout that season. My hope is to make the year meaningful as you discover topics and Scriptures themed for each season.

Season of Provision represents **Harvest**—that annual season of gathering, bounty, blessing, and provision. This set of writings deals primarily with the provision of God upon our lives and the bountiful harvest that comes to the person who follows God's Word and His will. I hope these words will be water to your soul and salve to your wounds.

Walk with me through God's *Season of Provision*, claiming and embracing the promises of the One whose heart beats to meet your need and be your supply.

"I will make them and the area around My hill a blessing: I will send down showers in their season—showers of blessing. The trees of the field will give their fruit, and the land will yield its produce; My flock will be secure in their land. They will know that I am the Lord when I break the bars of their yoke and rescue them from the hands of those who enslave them.

"They will no longer be prey for the nations, and the wild animals of the land will not consume them. They will live securely, and no one will frighten them. I will establish for them a place renowned for its agriculture, and they will no longer be victims of famine in the land. They will no longer endure the insults of the nations.

"Then they will know that I, the Lord their God, am with them and that they, the house of Israel, are My people." This is the declaration of the Lord God. "You are My flock, the human flock of My pasture, and I am your God." This is the declaration of the Lord God.

Ezekiel 34:26–31

CHAPTER 1

DON'T GIVE UP BEFORE YOUR HARVEST COMES IN
WORDS OF PROVISION FROM GALATIANS 6:7-9

MOST PEOPLE TODAY would probably agree one of the most trying things to do is wait for something. With just a click of a button, I can purchase anything from groceries to a new car—why go to a store? The most visited restaurants in our nation are not ones where you sit down to have a meal. They are the ones with a drive-through window where you can pick up your meal and eat while you drive. Computer chip manufacturers are constantly looking for ways to make our microprocessors faster and able to handle even more information then ever. Where does it stop? When will it end?

But despite a world that seems to be spinning faster and faster, there is one profession where the proccess cannot go any faster—farming. The farmer can use computers to do his paperwork. He can even use automatied sprinkling systems and high-tech combines. But he must still wait for the seeds to germinate, sprout, grow, and ripen. It takes time to reap a harvest.

Yet you rarely hear farmers saying things like, "Well, if I had known it was going to take six months for that seed to grow, I would have been a lawyer instead." A farmer knows better than the rest of us that patience, confidence, and faith are required when you are waiting on your harvest to come in.

> *Do not be misled: No one makes a fool of God. What a person plants, he will harvest. The person who plants selfishness, ignoring the needs of others—ignoring God!—harvests a crop of weeds. All he'll have to show for his life is weeds!*
>
> *But the one who plants in response to God, letting God's Spirit do the growth work in him, harvests a crop of real life, eternal life.*
>
> *So let's not allow ourselves to get fatigued doing good. At the right time we will harvest a good crop if we don't give up, or quit.*
>
> Galatians 6:7–9, MSG

FOUR LAWS OF SOWING AND REAPING

There are four laws attached to this principle of sowing and reaping. They are true in the natural world with literal seeds, and they are true in spiritual things as well.

1. We reap what we sow.

God instituted the law of seedtime and harvest, the law of sowing and reaping. "As long as the earth endures, seedtime and harvest, cold and heat, summer and winter, and day and night will not cease" (Gen. 8:22). When God created the first living thing, He gave it the ability to grow and multiply through the seed.

Your life began by the seed principle. And every act of your life since your birth has also operated this way, springing from the good seeds or bad seeds you have sown—whether or not you were consciously aware of your seed planting.

This principle continues today. To overcome life's problems, to reach your potential, and to see your life become fruitful (in your health, finances, spiritual renewal, family, your entire being), you must follow God's law of sowing and reaping. You must sow the seeds of God's promises (His Word) into the soil of your need.

We must daily take an inventory of our harvest, an inventory of our lives. First, we need to be honest with ourselves and before God when we answer this question: What kind of seeds am I sowing—into my marriage, my children, my church, my finances, my attitude, my job? Then, we must answer this question: Are the things I'm sowing producing positive or negative things in my life?

Are you reaping bad attitudes and habits? Are you reaping poor discipline? Are you reaping a weak spiritual life? The only way to change what you are harvesting is to plant different seeds. We will always get back the product of the seeds we sow!

2. We reap in multiples of what we sow.
Whatever we sow will be multiplied when we reap. That's why it takes more energy to bring in the harvest than it does to plant the seeds. It's scary to think that our troubles can multiply, but so can our blessings! It's our choice.

The reason we reap in multiples of what we sow is simple: *seeds produce more seeds!* When you put one orange seed into the ground, it will eventually grow into a tree filled with hundreds of oranges. And within each orange, there will be another five or six seeds. Just one seed can easily birth thousands more. Whether your fruit is good or bad depends on what you have sowed. Even Jesus promised the multiplication of our seed: "Give, and it will be given to you; a good measure—pressed down, shaken together, and running over—will be poured into your lap" (Luke 6:38).

> ONE PERSON GIVES FREELY, YET GAINS MORE. ANOTHER WITHHOLDS WHAT IS RIGHT, ONLY TO BECOME POOR.
> (PROVERBS 11:25)

3. We reap in a different season than we sow.

The Bible tells us that Isaac planted crops in the land during a famine. And the very same year, he reaped a hundredfold increase because the Lord blessed him (Gen. 26:12–13). Isaac didn't wait around until the committee told him conditions were suitable for planting. He went right out there in the middle of a famine, with people dying of starvation, when everything looked like a desert—and planted seeds.

There were people probably mocking and making fun of him—as people will do you when you give to the Lord out of your need. But those same people who had been making fun of him when he planted were probably standing in line at his house a few months later when the harvest came in.

God is the power behind the seeds you plant! He will spread a table in front of your enemies while you eat a seven-course meal and they eat their words. That's why you should always tithe, give offerings, read your Bible, pray, and minister to people—because in God's kingdom, it's always the right time to sow a seed. "Send your bread on the surface of the waters, for after many days you may find it. One who watches the wind will not sow, and the one who looks at the clouds will not reap" (Eccles. 11:1, 4). In other words, pay no attention to the negative elements that may be around you. Sow your seed in the face of the enemy, and God will cause blessing to be multiplied back to you.

Another person who reaped in a different season than when he sowed was Joseph. He was sold into slavery at age seventeen, and when he was thirty, Pharaoh promoted him (Gen. 41:50–52). Thirteen years after his captivity, he rose to power!

Even in his discontent—his "winter"—Joseph sowed seeds of faithfulness and loyalty to God, as well as seeds of trustworthiness and honesty to Pharaoh. And what did Joseph reap? After thirteen years, he was vindicated with Pharaoh. He married a beautiful wife and reaped two sons.

The first son was called Manasseh, which means, "making forgetful." Joseph said upon his birth, "God has made me forget all my hardship in my father's house" (Gen. 41:51). The second son was called Ephraim, which means "fruitfulness." Joseph said upon his birth, "God has made me fruitful in the land of my affliction" (Gen. 41:52).

When the blessing comes, it will be so overwhelming, you'll forget the time you spent waiting. Hallelujah!

Joseph also reaped vindication with his brothers. Joseph declared to them, "You planned evil against me; God planned it for good" (Gen. 50:20). God will take what the devil means for harm and use it for good if you'll keep sowing in faith, believing the harvest will come in. "Those who sow in tears will reap with shouts of joy" (Ps. 126:5).

4. We can change the reaping only by changing the sowing.

There are three distinct emotions we must not fall prey to when examining our harvest. They will not only get us into further trouble but will undermine our ability to reap a harvest of blessing.

> **Emotion 1: Transfer** — "It's not my fault."
> **Emotion 2: Irresponsibility** — "It's not my responsibility."
> **Emotion 3: Victimization** — "Nothing ever works for me."

These three attitudes open the door for the devourer—the seed-eater. The enemy will steal your seed if you give into that kind of negativity. We must let the Lord be the Lord of the harvest. He's in control of the timing—we're not. He has promised us that we will reap big time if we don't quit or give up.

But we must be careful what we sow. We must sow seeds of love and loyalty to our spouse and our children. We must sow seeds of integrity, honesty, prayer, Bible reading, tithes, offerings, and alms-giving into our spiritual life. We must sow seeds of care and concern into our relationships. We must not give up while doing the right thing. We don't want to be those who shrink back; we want to be those who go forward. God has called us to come up and into what He has for us, not down and out of His will.

Whatever we plant, we will harvest. We can't blame anyone else but ourselves if we are not happy with what we're reaping. Only the one who sows can change what will be reaped—by sowing different seeds.

Any time is a good time to sow. The time is now. In fact, the future is now. Because what you will be eating six months from now will be whatever you sow now. Little blessing or great blessing—it's up to you. While God is the Lord of the harvest, He leaves it up to us as to how much seed we place in His hands. Investing with God is the smartest thing you could ever do for yourself or those around you. The return on what you place in His hands will not only bless you but will touch all of those within your sphere of influence. Not only will you reap on this side of heaven, you are making eternal investments that will last forever.

> *And now, God, do it again—*
> *bring rains to our drought-stricken lives*
> *so those who planted their crops in despair*
> *will shout hurrahs at the harvest,*
> *so those who went off with heavy hearts*
> *will come home laughing, with armloads of blessing.*
>
> Ps. 126:4–6, MSG

CHAPTER 2

UNDER THE CIRCUMSTANCES
WORDS OF PROMVISION FROM HABAKKUK 3:16-18

THE PROPHET HABAKKUK'S name means "embrace." It's a fitting name because through his life and writings, we have a portrait of someone who when faced with dire circumstances, rather than giving up, "embraced" God in the midst of it all.

The Babylonian kingdom was on the move, and they were moving against everybody—including the apostate southern kingdom of Judah, of which Habakkuk was a part. When King Nebuchadnezzar of Babylon invaded Judah, he took a significant number of captives with him to Babylon—among whom were the prophet Daniel and his three friends, Shadrach, Meshach, and Abednego.

A few years later, the Babylonian army invaded Jerusalem again and ransacked the temple, this time taking 10,000 Jewish captives back with them—among whom was the prophet Ezekiel. When King Zedekiah attempted to free Judah from Babylonian occupation eleven years later in

586 BC, Nebuchadnezzar was so mad, he laid full siege to Jerusalem, burned the temple, totally destroyed the city, and brought back to Babylon as captives all of the remaining inhabitants of Jerusalem.

Habakkuk lived through most or all of this terrible time of Judah's judgment.

Yet amidst all of these terrible things, Habakkuk wrote something the apostle Paul would later quote in two of his letters: "the just shall live by his faith" (Hab. 2:4, NKJV). It is by faith we not only live but survive! If Habakkuk had written based on his circumstances, he would have never uttered these now famous words.

We must live by faith! Faith in God, in miracles, in prayer, in His Word. Faith that God can at any time transcend the ordinary and make it extraordinary. Our entire Christian existence is a walk of faith—from the day you had faith in the blood of Jesus to save you until the day your faith is rewarded when you go to live with the Lord forever.

Look at Habakkuk's faith declaration:

> *I heard, and I trembled within;*
> *my lips quivered at the sound.*
> *Rottenness entered my bones;*
> *I trembled where I stood.*
> *Now I must quietly wait for the day of distress*
> *to come against the people invading us.*
> *Though the fig tree does not bud*
> *and there is no fruit on the vines,*
> *though the olive crop fails*
> *and the fields produce no food,*
> *though there are no sheep in the pen*
> *and no cattle in the stalls,*
> *yet I will triumph in the Lord;*
> *I will rejoice in the God of my salvation!*
>
> *Habakkuk 3:16–18*

In others words, "Under the circumstances, I'm going to praise God anyway!"

If you're like me, you've had times—maybe even now—when you've walked around your spiritual property and surveyed the situation, and it's not good. The trees in your yard have no blossoms or fruit. The grape vines have no grapes. Your fields are barren and the seeds you planted are just lying there on the parched soil. Last year at this time they were full of grain, but not this year. Your flocks have disappeared. Your barns are empty of livestock. Now all that you own is nowhere to be seen. All that you've invested time and resources in seems to be gone. And you return home to an empty house, to a darkened room, with no one there but you and your thoughts.

You wonder what went wrong. Where did you miss it?

But then—call it crazy—something begins to well up inside of you, and you lift your voice and say, "God, I was counting on things being different, but they're not. Nevertheless, I want You to know that in spite of everything that hasn't happened, I love You! I worship You, I give you glory and honor. I thank You for my salvation! As Habbakuk said, 'I will rejoice in the God of my salvation!'"

It's insane to the unbeliever for us to do such a thing. But God's Word and experience has taught us to go ahead and give Him the glory. Go ahead and find joy in your circumstances, because this thing isn't over yet. God's not finished. God hasn't moved away from you. The joy of the Lord is going to be your strength!

We do not depend upon everything going our way to keep faith in God or to be faithful to Him. Real Christianity remains ever true despite external developments. If your relationship with God is real, you will love Him when the sun is shining as well as when it's raining.

> WHOM DO I HAVE IN HEAVEN BUT YOU? AND I DESIRE NOTHING ON EARTH BESIDE YOU.
> (PSALM 73:25)

I think God needs to hear us from time to time saying something like, "You know, God, I'm believing You for this, but if it doesn't happen, I'll love you anyway! I trust in Your timing, Your provision, and Your care!"

WHEN TROUBLE COMES, REJOICE!

How many times have we said, "Well, under the circumstances, I guess I'm all right," in a tone that's not too believable? Wouldn't it be great if we could remove from our vocabulary the words "under the circumstances"? Because such words give mental and emotional power to the circumstance!

Our response should be something like, "I'm in the middle of some stuff right now I don't understand, but I'm praising God because He's with me and strengthening me from the inside out in the midst of it all. He's in control." Despite any circumstances, what if we said, like Habakkuk, "I will rejoice in the God of my salvation!" Do we praise the Lord based on who He is, or on how easy our circumstances are? Is our praise based on a relationship with God, or is it based on what He gives us?

What do you do when trouble comes? Do you toil and fret, or do you begin to worship the Lord and rejoice in the God of your salvation? The Hebrew word used for "rejoice" is an interesting one. It is a verb that literally means "to spin around with intense emotion."

Although Habakkuk's circumstances were less than desirable, he was dancing for joy over his relationship with the Lord. If the Church of the Lord Jesus Christ studied all of the passages in Psalms on giving God praise—and lived them out—our worship would be the most exciting thing this world has ever seen. No wonder Psalm 149 instructs us to praise Him in dance. When people see that even though everything looks as if it's going wrong, we get up and jump with joy in the Lord anyway, that will preach more than any sermon ever could. Live out the joy!

While you await your ultimate victory and deliverance, go on and rejoice in the Lord. Even though there may not be any visible or external signs of a change, put your trust in Him. He will see you through it and on to the other side of it. Worship and rejoice in the Lord no matter what is (or isn't) happening at the moment.

Habakkuk went on to praise God in advance for His deliverance: "Yahweh my Lord is my strength; He makes my feet like those of a deer and enables me to walk on mountain heights!" (Hab. 3:19). The deer or gazelle in that part of the world is known for its fleetness and surefootedness on rough terrain. It is said that even a greyhound is liable to be killed by overexertion in pursuit of one. When we find ourselves in the rocky cliffs of hard times or climbing a slippery slope, our faith in God will make every rough place smooth beneath our feet, straightening every crooked path we must travel. He will give us the feet of a deer to travel into the heights.

> **DELIGHT YOURSELF IN THE LORD, AND I WILL MAKE YOU RIDE OVER THE HEIGHTS OF THE LAND. (ISAIAH 58:14)**

The words, "He makes my feet like those of a deer and enables me to walk on mountain heights," are also a picture of triumphing over the enemy of our souls. We can say with confidence and assurance: "Lead me to the Rock that is higher than I" (Ps. 61:2, NKJV). In other words, your faith in God and your rejoicing in your relationship with Him will help you rise above your circumstances to an out-of-the-way place where the enemy cannot touch you! Your faith will climb the heights no matter how narrow the trail.

God has a secure and safe place for you. The enemy can only sit and watch as you climb higher and higher and higher.

You may feel like your whole life has been one big negative circumstance after another. But something of substance is released in us and in the spirit realm when we praise God in spite of our circumstances. It does something on the inside of us.

So whatever you're going through, get up and praise Him! Jump up and down and twirl around with great joy in your heart because God is going to get you out and cause you to walk on mountain heights. The Lord is not finished; He's only just begun. God has not forgotten you. He will cause you to rise above this circumstance. His joy is your strength.

People might say, "You're crazy," but go ahead and praise Him with everything you've got. You've learned the secret: *circumstances change, but God does not!*

ESCORT DOUBT OUT THE DOOR
WORDS OF PROVISION FROM ACTS 9:36-42

CHAPTER 3

ONE OF THE MOST INSIDIOUS TACTICS of the enemy is to attack us with doubt. It can be doubt about anything—doubting the Lord, doubting that our prayers will be answered, doubting others, even doubting ourselves. Doubt and unbelief, like fear, can be a demonic spirit. The subtle lies of the enemy can come through a variety of sources to chip away at our faith.

Can you identify with that?

There's a great passage of Scripture that shares with us a valuable truth when it comes to dealing with the voices of doubt and unbelief. If we can learn the simple truths contained in these verses, we can walk in the light and power of God's Word with our resolve intact and our faith at mountain-moving proportions.

> *In Joppa there was a disciple named Tabitha, which is translated Dorcas.*

She was always doing good works and acts of charity. In those days she became sick and died. After washing her, they placed her in a room upstairs.

Since Lydda was near Joppa, the disciples heard that Peter was there and sent two men to him who begged him, "Don't delay in coming with us." So Peter got up and went with them. When he arrived they led him to the room upstairs. And all the widows approached him, weeping and showing him the robes and clothes that Dorcas had made while she was with them.

Then Peter sent them all out of the room. He knelt down, prayed, and turning toward the body said, "Tabitha, get up!" She opened her eyes, saw Peter, and sat up. He gave her his hand and helped her stand up. Then he called the saints and widows and presented her alive. This became known throughout all Joppa, and many believed in the Lord.

Acts 9:36–42

The New King James Version translates verse 40, "But Peter put them all out, and knelt down and prayed." Sometimes you need to put everyone out in order to get down and pray! When the voices of doubt and unbelief are weeping and crying because your answer to prayer hasn't come—when the voices of doubt and unbelief are encouraging you to join them and cry over your situation—that's the time to put them all out!

The disciples were weeping over Dorcas's death, failing to remember that God can resurrect anyone and anything—even you, even your dreams, even your heart's desires.

There are always people nearby who will be quick to get out their mourning gear and go to crying and wailing over your situation. They say things like, "Well, I knew things would end up this way," or "Well, you might as well face the facts; it's not going to happen."

You should examine the company you keep. Are they mourners, crying over something as if there's no hope left, or are they people of faith who will help you escort doubt out and then get down to pray and allow God to move? You must learn to refuse negative junk from other people. Words are powerful. Words that wear on you become the words you wear!

Our God is the Lord over the living and the dead. When you have a dead situation in your life, all you need to do is escort the doubt right out the door, get down on your knees, and let God breathe life into you and your dream again. He gave it to you, didn't He? So why should He not want to see it come to pass in your life?

God is for you, not against you.

Doubt and hopelessness will keep chipping away at you as long as you let them. You have to determine not to let negative thoughts come through. Remember, there is nothing negative about God! God is not going to give you negative words (although he will sometimes give you corrective words). He will not give you words that would destroy what He's spent so much time building in you.

Faith flourishes in an atmosphere that's filled with God's praises. Your faith is fed when you have people in your life who will speak faith-filled words over you and to you.

Jesus had a similar situation to the one we were just reading about in Peter's life:

> *While He was still speaking, someone came from the ruler of the synagogue's house, saying to him [Jairus], "Your daughter is dead. Do not trouble the Teacher." But when Jesus heard it, He answered him, saying, "Do not be afraid; only believe, and she will be made well."*
>
> *When He came into the house, He permitted no one to go in except Peter, James, and John, and the father and mother of the girl. Now all wept and mourned for her; but He said, "Do not weep; she is not dead, but sleeping." And they ridiculed Him, knowing that she was dead. But He put them all outside, took her by the hand and called, saying, "Little girl, arise." Then her spirit returned, and she arose immediately. And He*

> "BELIEVE THAT YOU HAVE RECEIVED THEM, AND YOU SHALL HAVE THEM." (MARK 11:24)

commanded that she be given something to eat. And her parents were astonished, but He charged them to tell no one what had happened.

Luke 8:49–56, NKJV

Notice verse 54: "But He put them all outside." Guess who Peter learned His ministry strategy from? Jesus! Jesus put them all outside, and Peter, James, and John were there to see it firsthand.

Something tells me that if it worked for Jesus, it will work for us. We need to remove hopeless mourning that doesn't give God a place to move. We need to escort doubt out the door!

When Jesus put out the doubters that day at Jairus' house, Peter learned an important truth: *an atmosphere of unbelief is not conducive to the faith that sees miracles!* Peter then did something we should do as well—he spent time in prayer!

In answer to Peter's prayer, Dorcas opened her eyes, looked at him, and then sat up. Giving her his hand, Peter raised her up. Then, calling all the believers, he presented her alive to them!

Many people believed on the Lord because of this. People of faith will have signs and wonders following them that will become, as the Scriptures teach, a testimony to the power of God and thereby a means of evangelism.

GOD WILL RESURRECT YOU

There are times when even those closest to you won't encourage what you do for God. In fact, John 7:1-9 tells us that Jesus' own brothers did not believe in Him—not until after His death and resurrection (Acts 1:14). There will be times when those closest to you—even your own family—won't believe in your confession. When that is the case, you don't have to be mean but you do need to show their negative comments to the door and put them out!

You must guard your heart and mind in Christ Jesus! Feed your faith by reading God's Word and repeating His promises every day of your life. God has given you the power to take authority over every thought and make it subject to Him and His will—over every negative thought, over every fiery dart of doubt, over every spirit of fear, over every panic attack.

"For God has not given us a spirit of fearfulness, but one of power, love, and sound judgment" (2 Tim 1:7). The Greek word for "sound judgment" can also be translated "safe thinking." Yes, God has given us "safe thinking"—the kind of thinking that says, "I'm letting all of this negativity go in one ear and out the other." The kind of thinking that says, "If God is for me, who can be against me?"

> **THE LORD IS FOR ME;
> I WILL NOT BE AFRAID.
> WHAT CAN MAN DO TO ME?
> (PSALM 118:6)**

You live with the choices you make! You are in control of your destiny to a great degree. You can be positive or negative. You can speak life or death over yourself and over your situation. The only person you are destined to become is the person you decide to be!

Oh, sure, there will always be detractors. There will always be people who disagree with you and who think you're doing the wrong thing. There will always be plenty of mourners around at the first sign of trouble or the first hint of a defeat.

You must have the courage to put them all out so that you can get down on your knees and say, "God, have your way. Heal me, save me, fill me—Lord God, touch and restore me—You alone can resurrect this situation!"

As Charles Spurgeon said, "Faith goes up the stairs which love has made, and looks out the window which hope has opened."

WHEN YOU'RE SCRAPING THE BOTTOM OF THE BARREL

WORDS OF PROVISION FROM 1 KINGS 17:8-16

CHAPTER 4

THIS STORY TAKES PLACE sometime around the late ninth century BC. Israel was living under its most wicked king, Ahab. God decided to respond to Ahab's wickedness through the prophet Elijah, who said the people should worship the Lord God and not the demon god, Baal. Because of Israel's disobedience, God told them (through Elijah) that the rain would cease for three and a half years. Not only was this a punishment for sin; it cut to the core of a false religion that claimed Baal controlled the rains and was responsible for successful crops. Elijah's prophetic word challenged this evil thinking, and the resulting drought proved that the Lord God of Israel was in control of the weather and everything else.

One of the ways God sustained Elijah through this period of drought was through a poor widow who was willing to give all she had to keep "God's man" alive. She gave out of her need to honor God—and ended up blessed in the process.

Then the word of the Lord came to him: "Get up, go to Zarephath that belongs to Sidon, and stay there. Look, I have commanded a woman who is a widow to provide for you there." So Elijah got up and went to Zarephath. When he arrived at the city gate, there was a widow woman gathering wood. Elijah called to her and said, "Please bring me a little water in a cup and let me drink." As she went to get it, he called to her and said, "Please bring me a piece of bread in your hand."

But she said, "As the Lord your God lives, I don't have anything baked—only a handful of flour in the jar and a bit of oil in the jug. Just now, I am gathering a couple of sticks in order to go prepare it for myself and my sin so we can eat it and die."

Then Elijah said to her, "Don't be afraid; go and do as you have said. Only make me a small loaf from it and bring it out to me. Afterwards, you may make some for yourself and your son, for this is what the Lord God of Israel says: 'The flour jar will not become empty and the oil jug will not run dry until the day the Lord sends rain on the surface of the land.'"

So she proceeded to do according to the word of Elijah. She and he and her household ate for many days. The flour jar did not become empty, and the oil jug did not run dry, according to the word of the Lord He had spoken through Elijah.

1 Kings 17:8–16

Elijah had been living by a creek where God had provided water for him to drink and had sent ravens to him twice a day with bread and meat during the famine. God had been teaching Elijah that He would provide for his every need—and to trust only in Him. Now God was going to use Elijah to teach this to someone else.

In the midst of the widow's dire circumstances, Elijah asked for whatever was left to be given to him first. Can you imagine such a request? But it was God asking her through him. It was God wanting her to place her trust in His word for her situation. God heard the scraping of the bottom of the barrel, too!

Elijah reassured the woman that her flour and oil would not run out as long as there was famine in the land. So the widow gave her all without asking where the next meal was coming from.

She found an important truth: in making God's will her first concern, He made her need *His* first concern! God saw to it that her supply of flour and oil continued until He sent rain on the earth.

We cannot go wrong giving to God! And each time we do, we learn by experience some valuable action plans we can put into practice:

1. Watch God meet your need in the middle of a drought!
God is not moved by the surrounding conditions that would normally hinder us. He controls the sun, the stars, the seas, and your situation! In fact, droughts can have a positive effect upon us as believers in Jesus Christ. They prove to us again and again God's omnipotence and His ability to meet our needs even under the most adverse circumstances. They show us how very much He loves us. He will not let us die in the desert!

2. Exchange the seen for the unseen!

God required of the widow all she had left to give. All that she could see, all that she was certain of, God asked her for. And she complied. In the giving of her all, miracle-working power was released. God proved to her that *He* was the source of blessing and provision, not what was in the barrel or the jug! Through her faith He was working a miracle on her and her son's behalf. In exchanging the seen for the unseen, she learned to walk into the unknown, trusting God for everything.

> FOR WHAT IS SEEN IS TEMPORARY, BUT WHAT IS UNSEEN IS ETERNAL.
> (2 CORINTHIANS 4:18)

Do we spend more time looking into the barrel or the jug than we do praising God daily for providing and meeting our needs? It is our human nature to trust in what is in the barrel, but God wants our spiritual nature to take over and trust in Him—because He is the one who fills the barrel! Our sufficiency is in Jesus Christ. We need to begin to live like the barrel is full, like the oil is running over, and like He intended us to live!

3. Don't ask questions—just believe!

The text does not mention that the widow questioned Elijah as to where her next meal was coming from. She didn't worry, she didn't seem to doubt, she didn't whine and complain, she didn't cry, and she didn't ask questions! She simply believed.

Jesus, in His rebuke of Satan, said, "Man must not live on bread alone but on every word that comes from the mouth of God" (Matt. 4:4). This woman was living off the Word! She was sustained by the Word of the Lord! God had given her a promise, and He is the Promise-keeper. May God help us all learn to stop asking so many questions and take Him at His Word.

4. Give Him something to multiply!

The widow could have told Elijah "no," eaten her last bit of bread, and died. But what little she had, she gave. And God began to go to work. She gave God something to multiply.

It is amazing how many people want God to do something for them but they don't give Him anything to work with. They want

God's blessings and provision, they want the barrel and the jug to be full, but they don't give Him something to multiply. I've learned that when you're at the end of your resources, you need to give anyway! You and I will never, ever go wrong giving out of our need to God.

5. God's miracle will last as long as you need it to!

The Lord provided for the widow's need until the rains came and allowed the soil to produce crops again. And He will see to it that your miracle lasts until the rains come again and water your thirsty soul.

Don't be afraid that He will stop looking after you. He can't and He won't. Why would He send His Son, Jesus Christ, to die for your sins if He didn't love you and want to help you? As you daily give yourself and your situation to God, you will see His provision at every turn. You don't have to keep looking in the barrel or eyeing the jar of oil.

It will be there because *He* is there in the midst of your situation.

PUT GOD FIRST

I do not believe that God filled the widow's house with barrels upon barrels of flour and jugs upon jugs of oil. As she used what she had, God daily filled the barrel with flour and the jug with oil. So it is with the power of God in our lives. As we use all that we have, He fills us up again through the indwelling presence of the Holy Spirit, His Word, and time spent with Him in worship. He daily meets our needs.

> GIVE ME NEITHER POVERTY NOR WEALTH. FEED ME WITH THE FOOD I NEED.
> (PROVERBS 30:8)

Jesus, when teaching us how to pray, said, "Give us today our daily bread" (Matt. 6:11). Not "yearly bread" or "weekly bread" or even "monthly bread," although some people want to live that way. He promised daily bread as we put Him first and minister to Him first. The power comes as you give out of what you have.

Jesus also taught us to freely give what we have freely received (Matt. 10:8). The more we give, we increase our own capacity for receiving more from Him.

Notice that Elijah told the widow to first make *him* something to eat before making something for herself and her son. When we seek first the kingdom of God and His righteousness, "all these things" are dispersed into our lives (Matt. 6:33). Our needs are met and the blessing comes as we put God first.

When you find yourself in the desert of drought and famine, see what's left in the barrel and in the jug of your supply. Whatever is there, give it all to Him. In exchange, He will bring an endless supply. He—not what's left—is your source. Take what's left and give it back to the Source, then watch what happens. Don't ask questions—just believe.

And the next time you reach into your supply and hear nothing but the sound of scraping at the bottom of your barrel, take heart, because He hears it too!

CHAPTER 5

GOD'S BED AND BREAKFAST
WORDS OF PROVISION FROM 1 KINGS 19:1-9

HAVE YOU EVER COME FROM A MIGHTY spiritual victory or a high point in your walk with the Lord, only to find yourself discouraged and depressed within a few days of your mountaintop experience? One minute you're God's man or woman of faith and power, and the next minute you're hiding out in a cave somewhere saying things like, "God, just take me home. I'm finished," or "I can't take this anymore."

Is this normal behavior? Or is it a sign that we're not as strong in the Lord as we claim to be?

Just as physical exercise and hard work can make us extra hungry, spiritual victories—which require spiritual warfare and battling the enemy—can also leave us spiritually hungry and in desperate need of spiritual sustenance and nutrition. But when it comes to spiritual things, we do not recognize the apparent needs as much as if they were natural needs, like food and rest.

Furthermore, we are so involved emotionally with a spiritual victory or battle that everything within us is flowing in the direction of achieving the victory, no matter what the cost. Then suddenly, after the Lord has given us the victory and the excitement begins to wear off, we feel kind of numb as we come back down to earth and the everyday-ness of our lives settles back in again.

We are often left with a feeling of being unspiritual. And, just like clockwork, the enemy capitalizes on this. We become discouraged with thoughts like, "What's the use?" and "By the way, Lord, where are you today?"

Don't think for a moment that God is not near when your feelings tell you otherwise. What you need is a little R&R at God's Bed and Breakfast. Then with a fresh perspective and an acute awareness that God will never abandon you, you go back into the fight to climb the next hill—the place that will be the setting for your next spiritual victory!

Case in point:

Ahab told Jezebel everything that Elijah had done and how he had killed all the prophets with the sword. So Jezebel sent a messenger to Elijah, saying, "May the gods punish me and do so severely if I don't make your life like the life of one of them by this time tomorrow!"

Then Elijah became afraid and immediately ran for his life. When he came to Beer-sheba that belonged to Judah, he left his servant there, but he went on a day's journey into the wilderness. He sat down under a broom tree and prayed that he might die. He said, "I have had enough! Lord, take my life, for I'm no better than my fathers." Then he lay down and slept under the broom tree.

Suddenly, an angel told him, "Get up and eat." Then he looked, and there at his head was a loaf of bread baked over hot stones and a jug of water. So he ate and drank and lay down again. Then the angel of the Lord returned a second time and touched him. He said, "Get up and eat, or the journey will be too much for you." So he got up, ate, and drank. Then on the strength from that food, he walked 40 days and 40 nights to Horeb, the mountain of God. He entered a cave there and spent the night.

1 Kings 19:1–9

Elijah had just celebrated one of the greatest spiritual victories of his life and ministry on Mount Carmel. God's fire fell upon the altar—a feat the heathen god, Baal, could not accomplish. Furthermore, Elijah killed the 450 prophets of Baal that had showed up to oppose the Lord God of Israel.

But when Elijah came down from Mount Carmel, he not only came down physically; he came down emotionally as well. And to add insult to injury (which the devil loves to do), Queen Jezebel had issued a death warrant for him because he had killed her demonic priests of Baal.

If any one will kick you when you're down, it will be hell itself.

GOD'S LOVE DOES NOT CHANGE

Straight from a spiritual victory, Elijah became discouraged and depressed. Trying to rest under a juniper tree, he confessed to God, "I have had enough, Lord. Take my life." Could this be God's man of faith and power? Yes, Elijah was still God's man of faith and power! Even after running for his life, even after whining for God just to kill him, he was still God's man, and God loved him—so much that he baked him a cake and had an angel deliver it!

God's love for us does not change when we go through times of discouragement. He is the God who does not change! *We* are the ones who are constantly changing and developing into the men and women God has called and purposed for us to be.

> "THE ETERNAL ONE OF ISRAEL DOES NOT LIE OR CHANGE HIS MIND."
> (1 SAMUEL 15:29)

When you're having a down day, don't think for a moment that God gets stressed out and has to take a nerve pill. Do you think God says, "Oh, no, what should I do now?" God knew how to take care of Elijah, and He knows how to take care of you.

The next time you feel yourself getting discouraged, the next time you feel yourself getting down, why don't you check into God's Bed and Breakfast and let Him bake you a cake! It'll get you to the next mountaintop.

"So he got up, ate, and drank. Then on the strength from that food, he walked 40 days and 40 nights to Horeb, the mountain of God" (1 Kings 19:8). Notice that Elijah went from his time of divine nourishment to the next "mountain of God." In between our mountaintop experiences, we often have moments of discouragement and despair. But God is there in the shadows, in the dark times, just like He was when you were on the mountaintop of a mighty victory.

Don't worry when the enemy comes to wear you down emotionally or make you feel discouraged. God will bake you a cake! He will spread a table in the wilderness right in front of your enemies! (Psalm 23:5). He will give you enough strength, enough grace, enough rest to get you to the next battle, to the next mountaintop. King David wrote, "I sought the Lord, and He answered me and delivered me from all my fears" (Psalm 34:4). David knew what it was to be discouraged in between spiritual victories. But he must have learned, just like Elijah, that God will bake you a cake, for he writes in the very same Psalm, "Taste and see that the Lord is good!" (34:8).

When God's children are discouraged in the place God has put them, they can take heart because through Jesus Christ and the ministry of the Holy Spirit, He will give them strength, grace, and encouragement, making them adequate for the task at hand. He has promised, "My grace is sufficient for you, for power is perfected in weakness" (2 Cor. 12:9).

The food He gives us in our weakest hour will sustain us on to the next mountaintop—even if it takes forty days to get there. In the strength of the Lord, we will go from glory to glory.

I will tell you that I've been through too many valleys, too many low times, too many depressed times, too many discouraging times, not to know that if it had not been for the Lord who was on my side, I would have been swallowed up. But He baked me a cake every time!

Sometimes that cake was the Word of God to my spirit, an encouraging word from a friend, or a song God had put in my heart. I am living proof of God's provision. There has never been a time when God greeted me with nothing. There has never been an instance when I've been in need that He's not shown up and turned the thing around. He was spreading a table in the wilderness for me every time.

Whether it's in the heat of battle or the hush of the night, God is ready to minister strength to us. His strength is the kind of strength that's perfected in our weaknesses. The kind of strength that gets stronger as we grow more and more dependent on Him.

> **HUMBLE YOURSELVES BEFORE THE LORD, AND HE WILL EXALT YOU.**
> **(JAMES 4:8)**

After a great spiritual victory or a long sustained spiritual high point, we can become emotionally vulnerable to discouragement and depression. We tend to let our defenses down after things get going good for any period of time, and we forget that the enemy is real, that he is committed to destroying us, intent upon doing whatever is necessary to discourage us or cause us to lose heart. But I'm here to tell you, the devil is a liar!

God's got a Bed and Breakfast you can check into when you get to feeling down, where He will provide you with food for the journey. God will bake you a cake like you've never had before!

Why don't you let God bake you a cake today? Why don't you stop running and hiding out under some tree somewhere? Why don't you stop believing the lie of the enemy that your last spiritual victory was your final one?

God wants to minister to your needs. Your discouragement and depression will disappear in His presence. One touch from the Lord and you'll be good as new. One taste of what He offers and you'll be running for days!

IT IS YOU
DAVID M. EDWARDS

Verse 1
You who moved the mountains
You who calmed the seas
You who made the heavens
You who first loved me

Chorus
It is You, You
Lord Jesus, it is You
It is You, You
Lord Jesus, it is You

Verse 2
You who bled and suffered
You who paid sin's price
You who died to save me
You who gave me life

Verse 3
You who sit in glory
You who'll never die
You who'll come back for me
It is You who'll split the sky

©2001 New Spring Publishing (ASCAP) / Nail Prince Music (ASCAP) Admin. by Brentwood-Benson Music Publishing, Inc. / Van Ness Press (ASCAP).

MERCY
DAVID M. EDWARDS

Verse 1
I'm at the end, I'm on my knees
Weighted down by all my need
I should have come when You first called
And yet Your love still broke my fall

Chorus
Lord, have mercy
Lord, have mercy on me, on me
Wash and cleanse me
Make me holy like Thee, like Thee
Have mercy

Verse 2
Obedience, not sacrifice
Is Your desire of all our lives
Surrender brings the deepest pain
Yet opens up heaven's rain

©2004 Mercy Seat Music / SelectSongsDotCom (ASCAP) Admin. by Music Services, Inc. / Van Ness Press (ASCAP) All Rights Reserved.

FOREVER I'LL PRAISE YOU
DAVID M. EDWARDS/CHUCK BUTLER

Verse 1
I'm standing here again
Your prodigal friend
Like so many times before
Come steal my sin away
Restore me, I pray
I'm so hungry, Lord, for more
Because You gave
Your life for me
As only You could do
I can see no other way
But to live this life for You

Chorus
When I lift my voice,
I'll sing to You
When I bow my head,
I'll honor You
'Cause You are my God
And I will praise You
When I raise my hands
Toward Your throne
I'll worship You and You alone
'Cause You are my God
And I forever will praise You

Verse 2
With each passing day
I discover new ways
Your mercy comes to me
You chase away my doubt
Your grace shows me how
In You I find my strength
Everywhere I go
And everything that I do
I want to be a living mirror
Reflecting nothing but You

Bridge
You are Lord of the heavens
And Lord of the earth
It amazes me
Your blood was my worth

©2002 New Spring Publishing, Inc. / Nail Prince Music (ASCAP) Admin. by Brentwood-Benson Music Publishing, Inc. / Van Ness Press (ASCAP)

MY REFUGE BE
MARGARET BECKER/DAVID M. EDWARDS/JOHN HARTLEY

Verse 1
All throughout my days
I will seek Your peace
Let me hear Your voice singing over me
And when my weary heart
Drives me to despair
In the shadows, Lord
Let me find you there

Chorus
Into you I will hasten
Into you I will lean
Light of the world, my only shelter
King of love, my refuge be
King of love, my refuge be

Verse 2
Friend of broken hearts
And all the lost
I will find my strength
In Your precious cross
And with every breath
That You give to me
May I glorify Your majesty

©2001 New Spring Publishing / Nail Prince Music (ASCAP) Admin. by Brentwood-Benson Music Publishing, Inc. / Van Ness Press (ASCAP) / WorshipTogether.com Songs (ASCAP) Admin. by EMI / Modern M Music (SESAC) Admin. by Music Services, Inc.

DAVID M. EDWARDS

David has been in ministry for fifteen years, and new songs of worship have been pouring out of him nearly all his life. He has worked with prolific songwriters such as Margaret Becker, Ginny Owens, Chris Eaton, Steve Hindalong, Greg Nelson, Natalie Grant, Matt Brouwer, Caleb Quaye, and John Hartley.

In 2003, he began his "Power to Worship Encounter," a popular seminar where attendees not only learn about the nuts and bolts of worship but experience God's presence as well. In 2005, he was awarded *Worship Leader* Magazine's "Best Scripture Song" Award for his song, "Create In Me," featured on his *Faithfully Yours: Psalms* project with Margaret Becker. Truly, this is only the beginning.

For more on David's music and ministry, contact: The Select Artist Group, P. O. Box 1418, LaVergne, Tennessee 37086, www.theselectartistgroup.com. Or visit www.davidmedwards.com.

Besides the three companion releases in the *Worship Through the Seasons* series, David's other books include a Psalms series—*Faithfully Yours*—as well as his signature work, *Worship 365*, and the *Holman CSB® Personal Worship Bible*, with more to come.

ACKNOWLEDGEMENTS

I wish to express my sincere appreciation to my publisher, David Shepherd, for being open to the things of God and open to me. To Ken Stephens, John Thompson, Jean Eckenrode, Jeff Godby, Lawrence Kimbrough, and the entire B&H family—my sincere thanks for all you've done for me.

To my literary agent, David Sanford, and the entire staff at Sanford Communications, Inc.—thank you so much for your guidance and perseverance. I would in particular like to thank my editor, Elizabeth Jones, for a phenomenal job and for working so quickly.

To my manager, Glenda J. McNalley, I wish to express my deep appreciation for her tireless efforts on my behalf and for her unwavering friendship.

To my beautiful wife, Susan, thank you for your love and standing by my side. *I love you!* To our wonderful blessings, Tara, Elyse, and Evan—Daddy loves you so much.

To my parents, Louis and Wanda Edwards, thank you for your "provision." To my brother, Daniel, thank you for always being a faithful friend.

GOD'S WORD...

THE HEART OF WORSHIP.

THE HEART OF BIBLE LEAGUE.

Help put God's Word into Action!

Just $4 places a Bible in the hands of someone waiting for His Word.

Let me tell you more about the incredible
worldwide ministry
of Bible League at
WWW.BIBLELEAGUE.ORG/DAVIDMEDWARDS

Bible League | 866-825-4636 (TOLL FREE)
WWW.BIBLELEAGUE.ORG

ALSO AVAILABLE FROM DAVID M. EDWARDS AND B&H PUBLISHING GROUP

FAITHFULLY YOURS: WORSHIPFUL DEVOTIONS FROM THE PSALMS
EACH BOOK INCLUDES A 4 SONG WORSHIP CD
- CREATE IN ME ISBN: 0-8054-4329-0
- ENTER HIS GATES ISBN: 0-8054-4330-4
- AS HIGH AS THE HEAVENS ISBN: 0-8054-4331-2

WORSHIP 365 ISBN: 0-8054-4367-3
DAVID'S SIGNATURE WORK ON WORSHIP

THE PERSONAL WORSHIP BIBLE ISBN: 1-58640-280-3
FEATURING THE HOLMAN CHRISTIAN STANDARD BIBLE®

WORSHIP THROUGH THE SEASONS
- ADVENT: SEASON OF PROMISE ISBN: 0-8054-4324-X
- HARVEST: SEASON OF PROVISION ISBN: 0-8054-4333-9
- EASTER: SEASON OF PASSION ISBN: 0-8054-4332-0
- PENTECOST: SEASON OF POWER ISBN: 0-8054-4334-7

Available at bookstores and online retailers everywhere, or at BHPublishingGroup.com

[springhillworship]

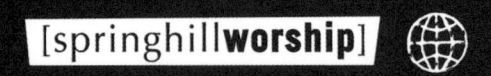

CHECK OUT THESE EXCITING NEW WORSHIP RELEASES
NEW worship music • FREE song downloads • BIBLE studies • Chord charts • Lyric sheets and more!

NEW WORSHIP SONGS BY:
Anadara, Carl Cartee, Detour 180, Billy Sprague, Tom Lane, Rick Cua and Scott Riggan!

ALSO FEATURING THE NEW RELEASE BY DAVID M. EDWARDS

WWW.SPRINGHILLWORSHIP.COM   enhanced CD